THE SUSTAINABLE DEVELOPMENT GOALS

The Sustainable Development Goals

Published by the United Nations
New York, New York 10017, United States of America

Copyright © 2017 United Nations
Illustration copyright © by YAK (Yacine Aït Kaci)
All rights reserved

ISBN: 978-92-1-101369-6
eISBN: 978-92-1-362512-5
Sales No: E.17.I.8
United Nations Publication

SUSTAINABLE
DEVELOPMENT
G🌀ALS

WHAT ARE THE
SUSTAINABLE DEVELOPMENT GOALS?

On 1 January 2016, the 17 Sustainable Development Goals (SDGs) of the 2030 Agenda for Sustainable Development — adopted by world leaders in September 2015 at a historic UN Summit — officially came into force. With these new Goals that universally apply to all, countries are mobilizing efforts to end all forms of poverty, fight inequalities and tackle climate change, while ensuring that no one is left behind.

The SDGs, also known as Global Goals, build on the success of the Millennium Development Goals (MDGs) and aim to go further to end all forms of poverty. The new Goals call for action by all countries, poor, rich and middle-income, to promote prosperity while protecting the planet.

They recognize that ending poverty must go hand-in-hand with strategies that build economic growth and address a range of social needs including education, health, social protection, and job opportunities, while tackling climate change and environmental protection.

For the Goals to be reached, everyone needs to do their part: governments, businesses, civil society and people like you. Join Elyx, the UN's first digital ambassador, as he explores the meaning of each of the Goals.

NO POVERTY

1

Ending poverty around the world is the first goal. Millions of people lack the basic resources to enjoy a decent life. Goal 1 will make sure that everyone has access to food, shelter, clothing, healthcare and education so they can fully participate in society. Being poor often also means lack of access to such essential things as social security, new technologies, property, control over land and financial aid, all of which this Goal seeks to correct. We may also need to help people touched by climate and other natural disasters as well as social and economic shocks.

END POVERTY
IN ALL ITS FORMS
EVERYWHERE

2

ZERO HUNGER

2

While there is food available to feed everyone, so many people, including children, still go hungry. Goal 2 focuses on addressing poor agricultural practices, food waste and environmental degradation to ensure no one goes hungry. We must improve the way that food is grown now and for the future without causing damage to nature. This can be done through support of small scale and local farming, providing more funds for the production of food, especially in poorer countries, and helping limit volatility in food prices.

**END HUNGER,
ACHIEVE FOOD SECURITY
AND IMPROVED NUTRITION
AND PROMOTE
SUSTAINABLE AGRICULTURE**

3

GOOD HEALTH AND WELL-BEING

3

When people are in good health, societies prosper. While a lot ha~~been done to reduce the impact of HIV/AIDS, malaria and other diseases in recent years, real progress can only be achieved wh~~everyone, including women and children, has access to good hea~~care. Goal 3 includes essential targets such as the reduction of maternal mortality and deaths of infants and children; promotio~~family planning; prevention and treatment of addictions; and hal~~ing the number of traffic accidents all over the world. There is ar~~urgent global need to put an end to epidemics, provide affordabl~~vaccines and essential medicines for all, cut the risk of chemical~~and biological pollution and the contamination of people. This go~~can't be achieved without increasing the number of doctors and nurses in the most vulnerable areas of the world.

**ENSURE HEALTHY LIVES
AND PROMOTE WELL-BEING
FOR ALL AT ALL AGES**

ELYX BY YAK

**QUALITY
EDUCATION**

Access to education can help lift people out of poverty, bring a deeper understanding of the world around us and provide better opportunities for everyone, including girls. Goal 4 is all about ensuring everyone has access to learn no matter who they are or where they are. Vulnerable people, including children in difficult situations, persons with disabilities and indigenous peoples must receive quality education. Goal 4 insists that all people be brought up to promote human rights, peace and non-violence so that we can coexist harmonious

**ENSURE INCLUSIVE
AND QUALITY
EDUCATION FOR ALL
AND PROMOTE LIFELONG
LEARNING**

ELYX BY YAK

5

GENDER
EQUALITY

5

Women and girls still suffer discrimination and violence - and that's half of the world's population! Goal 5 is about achieving gender equality, including equal access to education, health care and decent work, all of which can only benefit societies. Ending discrimination and violence against women and girls everywhere in the world, including forced marriage and female genital mutilation, are key to achieving this goal. We also need to ensure women and girls' full access to essential sexual and reproductive human rights. Women need to be able to own property, access financial services and new technologies and take part at all levels of the political, economic and public life of their communities. Increasing the number of women who become leaders, company managers and members of parliament in their countries is another essential part of this Goal.

ACHIEVE GENDER EQUALITY AND EMPOWER ALL WOMEN AND GIRLS

ELYX by YAK

6

CLEAN WATER AND SANITATION

There are billions of people all over the world without access to clean water and toilets, a human right that many of us take for granted. Water scarcity and inadequate sanitation have a huge cost, not least of all the number of people, especially children, who die from diseases every year. Water is essential for life, and therefore should not be polluted but rather be recycled and re-used by everyone. Goal 6 includes the protection and restoration of areas where water can be found such as forests, mountains, wetlands, rivers and lakes; helping local communities manage their water supply; ensuring that water is supplied fairly to all, and encouraging countries to work together for the common good in areas where water supply is shared across borders.

**ENSURE ACCESS
TO WATER
AND SANITATION
FOR ALL**

AFFORDABLE AND CLEAN ENERGY

7

We must provide affordable and reliable energy to the billions who still rely on wood and charcoal for cooking and heating. Goal 7 also underscores the need for clean and renewable energy to help combat climate change. Energy should be produced in a modern, cheap, reliable and viable way. It should be as clean as possible and come from pollution free sources such as sun and wind. This goal aims to support and expand the supply of modern forms of energy to developing countries and ensure that all countries work together to promote clean energy research and improve technology that will benefit people as well as the planet.

ENSURE ACCESS TO AFFORDABLE, RELIABLE, SUSTAINABLE AND MODERN ENERGY FOR ALL

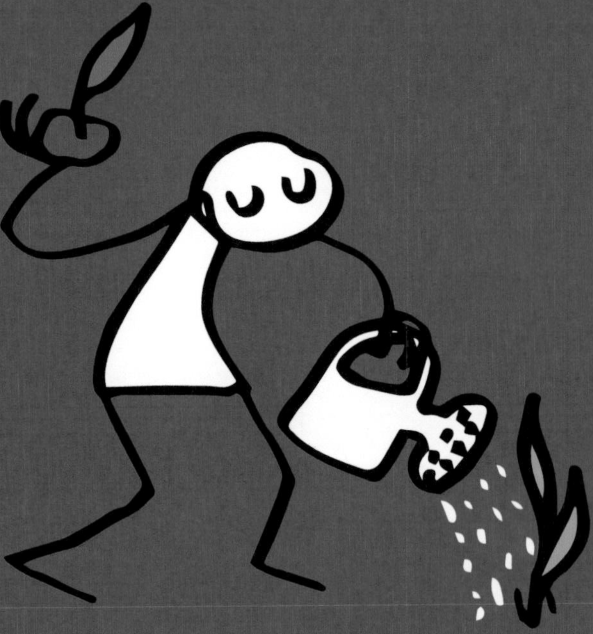

ELYX BY YAK

DECENT WORK AND
ECONOMIC GROWTH

8

With global unemployment on the rise, we need to find ways to create more jobs. Goal 8 calls for more jobs that not only provide decent pay b also stimulate the economy and provide equal opportunities for both m and women while protecting the environment. Providing work to every-body will increase personal wealth and thus make the economy stronge in each and every country. We must make sure that everybody, includin all women, men, young people and persons with disabilities can be employed and that everyone is paid equally for equal work. Increasing the number of small and medium sized companies that can employ people in productive jobs without harming the environment is also an important part of this goal. Together we must eradicate forced labour, modern slavery, human trafficking and child labour all around the worl

PROMOTE INCLUSIVE AND SUSTAINABLE ECONOMIC GROWTH, EMPLOYMENT AND DECENT WORK FOR ALL

9

INDUSTRY, INNOVATION
AND INFRASTRUCTURE

Goal 9, in simple terms, states that for a society to grow, it should encourage industries that bring opportunities to everyone while protecting the environment. These industries must also be supported by resilient infrastructure such as reliable transport as well as by technological innovation. Industries that employ people need to be given technological, financial and scientific support to allow them to succeed, especially in developing countries. Access for all to information and communications technology as well as affordable access to the Internet is essential.

BUILD RESILIENT INFRASTRUCTURE, PROMOTE INCLUSIVE AND SUSTAINABLE INDUSTRIALIZATION AND FOSTER INNOVATION

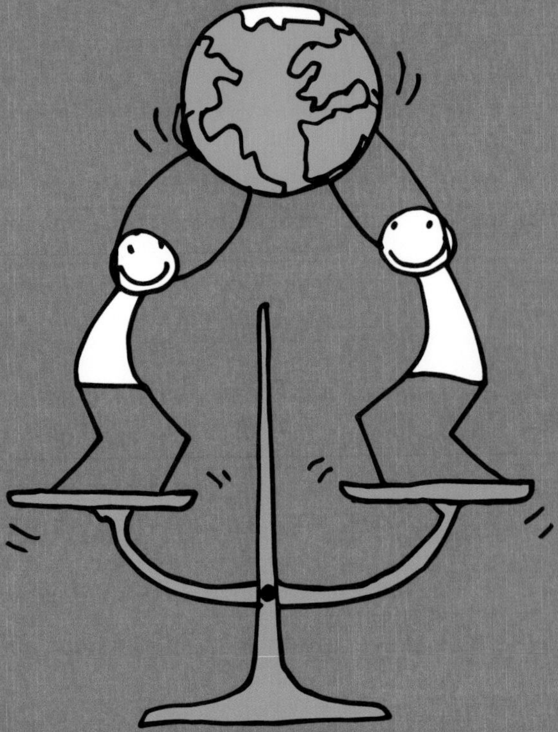

ELYX BY YAK

10

REDUCED
INEQUALITIES

10

For real improvements in a society, everyone needs to have access to opportunities that will let them grow as individuals. But this is not the case in many places where people face discrimination because of their gender, disability status, ethn or racial group, or background. Goal 10 seeks to make sure everyone everywhere has a chance to live a healthy and happ life. It is about reducing the inequalities between rich and poo people as well as among rich and poor countries. Developing countries need to have a greater say in international economi and financial systems and be supported through internationa aid. Safe and orderly migration of people is to be ensured.

REDUCE INEQUALITY WITHIN AND AMONG COUNTRIES

SUSTAINABLE CITIES
AND COMMUNITIES

11

Cities are lively hubs for ideas, commerce, culture, science, productivity and much more. But they face many challenges such as pollution, lack of basic services for many citizens, and declining infrastructure. Our cities and villages need to be clean and safe, with good housing and basic services like water and electricity. They also need clean, efficient transport systems and green areas that everyone can enjoy. People need to be protected from disasters and the effects of climate change. Important cultural and natural sites need to be preserved for all. We need to improve air quality and waste management while supporting developing countries in constructing better buildings with local materials.

MAKE CITIES INCLUSIVE, SAFE, RESILIENT AND SUSTAINABLE

12

RESPONSIBLE CONSUMPTION AND PRODUCTION

12 ∞

Goal 12 wants to make us think twice about the things we use, the waste we create, and how that impacts our planet. Changing our behaviour towards more sustainable actions such as recycling really makes a difference when everyone - that includes individuals, companies, governments - contributes. There are many little things we can all do to achieve this goal. Goal 12 aims to improve the quality of life of all people, and not just a few, everywhere on the planet.

ENSURE SUSTAINABLE CONSUMPTION AND PRODUCTION PATTERNS

ELYX BY YAK

13

CLIMATE ACTION

13

Our climate has always been changing, but in the past 200 years the changes have become more extreme because of human activity. Climate change is now affecting every country on every continent and the poorest and most vulnerable people are being affected the most. Goal 13 is about finding solutions like renewable energy and clean technologies to combat climate change. But it will take action from governments, the private sector and civil society to make a significant impact. It is urgent to educate people and raise their awareness of climate change in schools and through community outreach. Developing countries require financial resources to protect themselves against the effects of climate change. Support is needed for developing countries and small island developing States to help with the consequences of environmental change, with particular focus on women, young people, local communities and the disadvantaged.

TAKE URGENT ACTION TO COMBAT CLIMATE CHANGE AND ITS IMPACTS

14

LIFE BELOW WATER

14

Goal 14 is about protecting the oceans, seas and all their species.
Why? Because oceans provide food, medicines, biofuels and jobs
for millions of people. Taking good care of our oceans also helps us
address climate change. We need healthy oceans, and they need us
protect them! We must all work in particular to reduce plastic debris
that cause great damage to plant and animal life and endanger species. Some of the targets of Goal 14 consist in reducing marine acidi
controlling overfishing and illegal fishing to restore fish stocks, and
increasing protected marine and coastal areas around the world.
It strives to legally protect the oceans and seas through the United
Nations Convention on the Law of the Sea and assist developing cou
tries and small island developing States that are particularly affecte

CONSERVE AND SUSTAINABLY USE THE OCEANS, SEAS AND MARINE RESOURCES

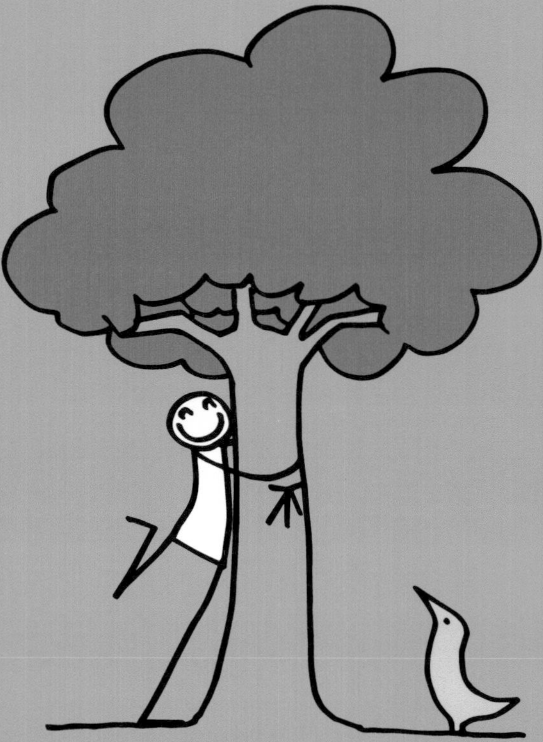

ELYX BY YAK

15

LIFE ON LAND

15

We are all part of the global ecosystem. Goal 15 is about making sure that we stop activities that threaten our global home. This includes deforestation, land degradation, and loss of animal and plant species. Nature contributes so much to people's lives and it is essential to protect it. This Goal calls for an urgent end to the killing and trafficking of protected species and increased spending to protect nature and assist developing countries in doing so. It also aims to educate people to respect the land and everything it gives us so that our children continue to enjoy nature in the future.

SUSTAINABLY MANAGE FORESTS,
COMBAT DESERTIFICATION,
HALT AND REVERSE LAND
DEGRADATION,
HALT BIODIVERSITY LOSS

ELYX by YAK

16

PEACE, JUSTICE AND STRONG INSTITUTIONS

16

Too many people experience war and violence. Goal 16 is about finding ways to make sure everyone lives in a peaceful society, where they can have access to justice, and don't have to live in fear. It strives to end abuse, exploitation, trafficking and all forms of physical or psychological violence against children and teenagers, women and men all around the world. It aims to ensure that small arms and light weapons are very tightly controlled. Together we must work towards ending corruption and bribery in public life; greatly reducing illegal flows of money and arms; returning stolen property to where it belongs, and combatting organized crime and terrorism. All people are encouraged to participate in the public life of their countries.

PROMOTE PEACEFUL AND INCLUSIVE SOCIETIES FOR
USTAINABLE DEVELOPMENT, PROVIDE ACCESS TO JUSTICE FOR
ALL AND BUILD EFFECTIVE, ACCOUNTABLE AND INCLUSIVE
INSTITUTIONS AT ALL LEVELS

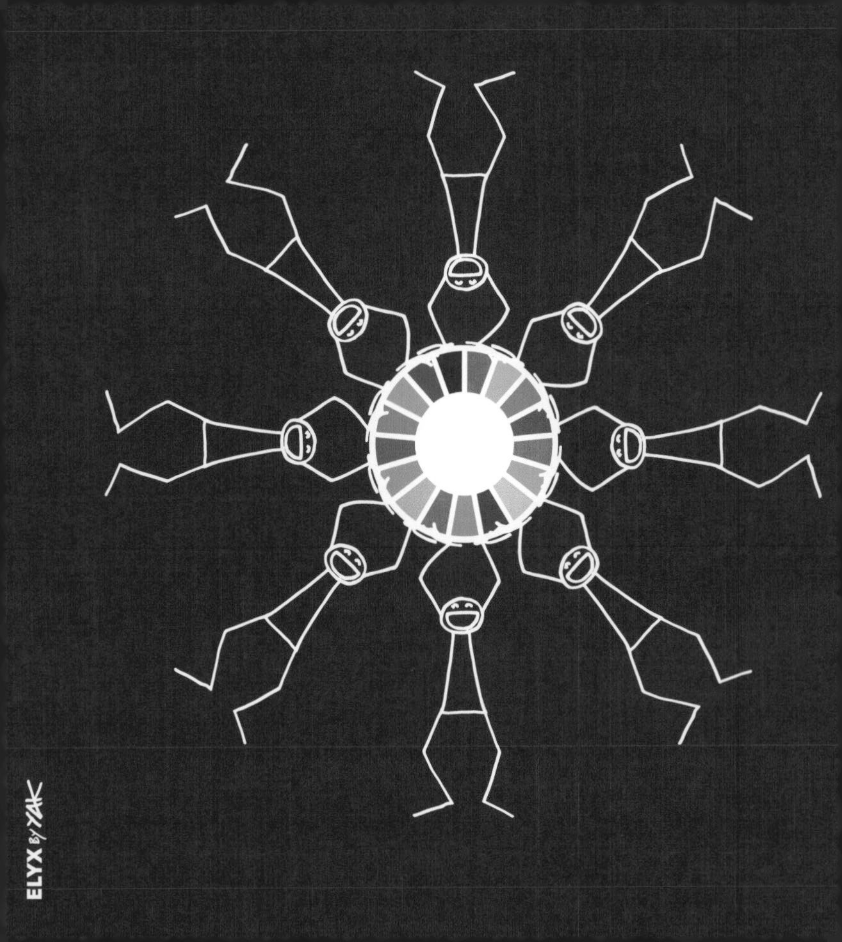
ELYX BY YAK

17

PARTNERSHIPS FOR THE GOALS

17

To make all the goals a reality will require the participation of everyone. That includes governments, the private sector, civil society organizations and people like you! The best part is that we don't have to work alone. If we join forces and partner we can get there faster and succeed on each goal. Developed countries must help developing countries with more assistance financially, scientifically and technologically, including aid to export more products internationally and to build their own local capacity. Developing countries should also be helped to reduce their debt so that they are enabled to better manage their future.

EVITALIZE THE GLOBAL PARTNERSHIP FOR SUSTAINABLE DEVELOPMENT

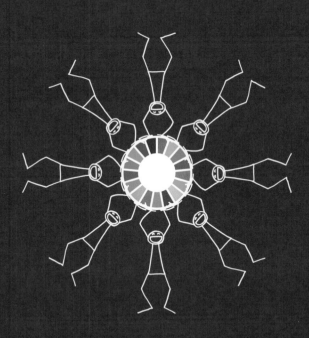